THE GAME & FISH MASTERY LIBRARY

SALMON

By S. G. B. Tennant, Jr.
Photography by Arie deZanger

WILLOW CREEK PRESS

Minocqua, Wisconsin

Published by Willow Creek Press
P.O. Box 147
Minocqua, Wisconsin 54548

Designed by Heather M. McElwain

For information on other Willow Creek titles, call 1-800-850-9453

Library of Congress Cataloging-in-Publication Data
Tennant, S.G.B.
    Salmon / by S.G.B. Tennant, Jr. ; photography by Arie deZanger.
      p.   cm. -- (The game & fish mastery library)
  ISBN 1-57223-184-X
  1.   Cookery (Salmon)   I. Title.   II. Series.
TX748.S24T46   1999
641.6'92--dc21   99-17057
                                         CIP

Printed in Canada

TABLE OF CONTENTS

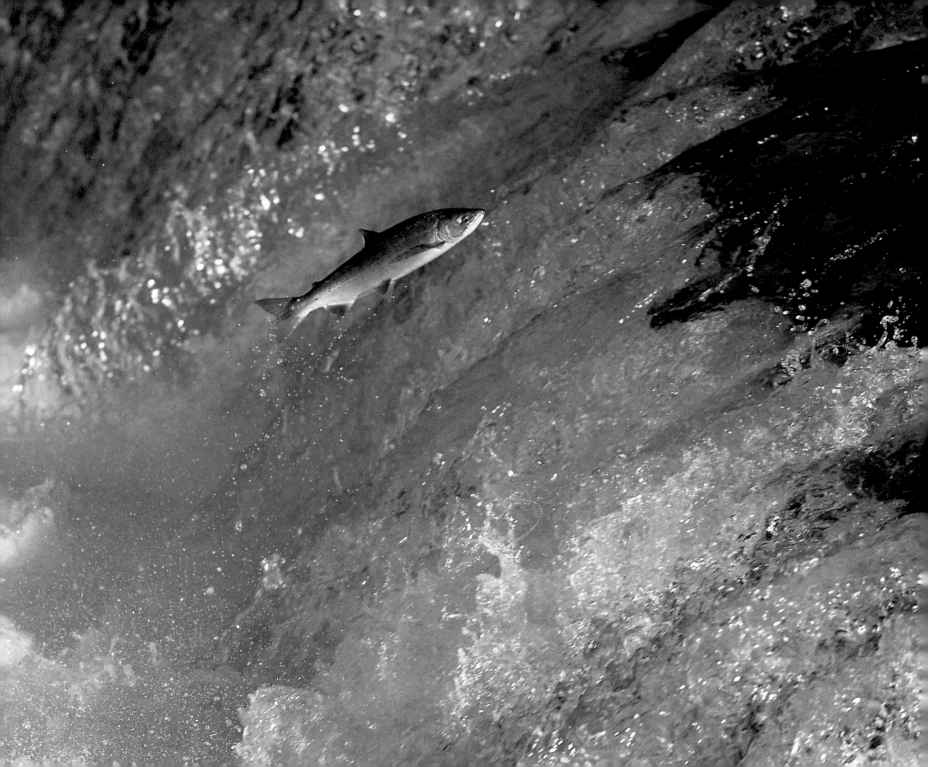

ACKNOWLEDGMENTS

The Atlantic Salmon Federation is leading the fight. Ask what you can do.

Atlantic Salmon Federation
St. Andrews, New Brunswick
Canada E0G 2X0
(506) 529-4581

We would like to express our gratitude to Kirk Avondoglio of Perona Farms [(800) 750-6190] for supplying the spectacular fresh salmon that brought these recipes to life.

Patio-Classic of Louisville Kentucky [(800) 585-4745] produces the barbecue grills used here in the backyard settings.

Calvin Klein Home provided dishware and glassware [(800) 294-7978].

Dansk provided dishware and table settings [(800) 293-2675].

Further information and supplies:

Polarica
105 Quint Street
San Francisco, California 94124
(800) GAME-USA

Czimer's Game and Sea Foods, Inc.
13136 W 159th Street
Lockport, Illinois 60441-8767
(708) 301-0500

INTRODUCTION

Of all of the fish in the ocean, the salmon probably means more things to more people than any other creature. This is true especially for me, since the few I've caught have been so few and so far between. Each one, I found to my utter joy, was encrusted with legend, folklore and a double-helping of half-truths.

In our kitchen, however, it has been a uniformly different tale. This is a fish to conjure and to celebrate, and you can do so without risking your reputation for veracity or creativity. No more trips to Scotland or the rivers of British Columbia. Salmon now come by the box-load from farms in Canada and New Zealand. The Scottish smoked cure rests beside the modern gravlax in supermarkets. The array is baffling and one has to wonder what the "ordinary" folks are having for dinner.

The salmon has been the plaything of chefs since they began to put roofs on kitchens. I remember the sunny gardens of Vienne, France where Fernand Point once ruled imperiously. His menu always contained the alluring but slightly mysterious "scallops" of salmon. Those were in the days before a sort of post-modern realism invaded the great kitchens, and there was no obligation to make a meal look like anything else. In those days a circular-shaped slice of salmon that contained just a hint of heaven required no further explanation.

The real challenge of this book has been selecting the recipes from the many spectacular presentations on which I have grown to rely. Those that show the fish across the spectrum of its charm got first nod. History and precedent were second.

The simple fact that almost everyone in America has tasted salmon at one time or another is not a guarantee of universal acceptance — except at the highest gastronomic level. For over thirty years Julia Child has cheerfully been beating the drum of French and American presentations of this great fish, and the markets and consumer demand have finally caught up with her, to the enormous benefit of us all.

In this effort it has been a great help to me to have the "fish savvy" insights of renowned photographer Arie deZanger. On location and in remote places I have watched Arie do engaging and artful photographs across a selection of food work that ranged from illustrations of the works of A. J. McClane to G.A. Escoffier.

I cannot mention Al McClane, my late colleague, without acknowledging his pioneering work in making fish a respectable subspecialty in the American food revolution. Chefs and restaurant-goers worldwide have benefited from his *Encyclopedia of Fish Cookery,* now sadly out of print, and his devotion to the splendor and dignity of gamefish.

There are two small fry who always demand and receive my special attention, and with great expectations for their future these pages are dedicated to Philadelphia and Elise, two of the brightest fish in the ocean.

Good Cooking!

— *S.G.B. Tennant, Jr.,*
Helena, Texas

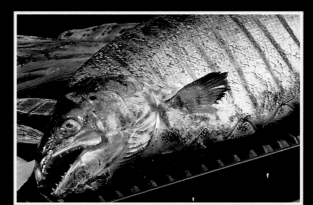

A long time before people were interested in sport fishing, salmon was the manna of the European world. The great fish tumbled out of every river that touched the Atlantic Ocean and onto the banquet tables of a grateful pagan elite. The great roast salmon, borne aloft on a flaming spit, became the symbolic festival food for ancient Irish kings and eventually the princes of Europe.

Today's great chefs serve the salmon habitually. Chef Charlie Trotter offers a Chicago variation in the form of Salmon Napoleon. Chef André Soltner glazes the great fish with a mustard mousse! Chefs from the ancien régime, Fernand Point and his French battalions, all offered "scallops du saumon" on their Sunday menus.

I believe it is the unique and sturdy flavor of the fish, occupying a gastronomic niche, if you will, that is so recognizable that it is used without embarrassment across the culinary spectrum. And in the modern day rush to display the great fish, even "classic" Italian cookery writers have offered a salmon or two without the slightest trace of irony at the fact that this fish never swam in Italian waters.

The two best of all salmon, the Atlantic and the king (or Chinook), are also the most adaptable in the kitchen. The Atlantic salmon can be grilled whole, or filleted into the gossamer translucenies of gravlax. The sturdy Pacific king produces bright red fillets whose character accommodates sauces that range from the piquant hollandaise to a subtle shrimp Nantua.

The salmon's rise to high status as food more or less paralleled its rise as a much sought-after object by the "sporting classes" in Olde Europe. There is barely a mention of this fish in pre-modern food writing by those such as Brilliat Savarin, Carême or Soyer. It wasn't until the latter 19th century, largely under the leadership of George Auguste Escoffier, that salmon was seen as a versatile and tasty marvel, sufficiently exclusive to be reserved for the "cultivated" palates.

But along the way to haute cuisine the salmon fell out of favor with the commoners. Trapped, netted, and distributed to the masses with increasing efficiency, by the 19th century Dickens was able to equate poverty with eating salmon and oysters. How things change! There was once such a glut of salmon that indentured servants bound for the New World had clauses in their contract limiting the number of salmon meals per week they would be fed.

Eventually the supplies ran out. Pollution of the great rivers of Europe and America drastically reduced the supply of the great fish. The bitter legacy of the industrial revolution is that fish became scarce wherever people had settled. The last fish in the Connecticut River died out by 1815, remembered fondly in the poetry of Longfellow, and in the traditional New England Independence Day dinner celebrated in these pages.

The Atlantic salmon from Scotland, smoked or not, ranks highest on everyone's taste chart, but the Irish want to fight about that, and the one-upmanship starts in, and carries on all the way down to the local fish tank.

If you have a wild fish in your kitchen, feel blessed. Anyone who has caught the real thing will insist very rightly that this fish is the best. Since enthusiasm is eighty percent of a good meal no further comment is needed. In terms of the farm-raised fish much that is complimentary should be said. These fish are of an extremely reliable character, and any fish under ten pounds bought in a market is likely farm raised and a most propitious prospect.

Pacific salmon come to market under a glittering array of "brand names," some even being packaged for various ethnic markets. King salmon spend the longest time (four to six years) in the ocean before returning to spawn and die, and perhaps because of this extended ocean time they have a flavor that is clearly the epicures' favorite of the Pacific fleet.

Down market slightly, the Coho, or silver salmon, is esteemed for the sport it provides; and the sockeye is lauded for its prolific abundance, even though only the introduced land-locked sockeye variety will readily take a hook.

All this, however, is changing faster than a salmon can be caught. Since the mid-1960s offshore commercial salmon harvesting has steadily reduced the stocks and threatened the fisheries. With the rivers damned up, and the oceans full of nets, the future seems bleak.

Yet hope is at hand. The Edwards dam across the Kennebec River in Maine is up for demolition, as are dozens more like it. In the mountains of New Zealand enterprising fish farmers have sockeye farms and established markets, and are now branching out to raise the popular king salmon.

There are millions of tons of salmon farm raised these days, in Norway, Canada and Scotland, and all of it of excellent table quality. Their product comes to market based on an annual crop, just like beef or chicken, and that's the reason so many market fish are in the 6- to 8-pound category. That's a two-year-old salmon.

None of this commercial enthusiasm would exist, of course, except for the soaring demand of the market and the modern transportation network. And that, in turn, is driven by the brilliant flavor and reliable texture of all salmon.

A good example of the adaptability of this fish is its original appearance in the folklore of Russia as the lowly peasant fish loaf, called a *kulebyaka*. Before the Bolshevik revolution the Russians caught Pacific salmon, mostly king salmon, and rolled them into a swept-up pastry to feed the hearty peasants.

Escoffier, the first modern chef, rescued this dish from mediocrity, conjured a bright velouté sauce, and spared no pains with the encrusted pastry case. In his hands the dish was reborn under the French name *coulibiac* and has been a standard in the haute cuisine repertoire ever since.

Similarly, many of the old peasant dishes have been revived recently, making a virtue out of what was once a necessity. It is still the custom in some of the great fishing lodges in Scotland, for instance, to offer both smoked salmon and the gravlax salmon at the same meal.

The gravlax is prepared following ancient rituals, as old as eating itself. The action of the sugar and salt effectively cure the meat, yet because of the gentle effect on the tissues, every nuance of flavor is preserved, only slightly enhanced by the dill. This old Swedish recipe is open to invention, and has been varied everywhere — including here, with the brown sugar that lends a delicate charm.

The arrival of the kitchen processor, only slightly less portentous than the contributions of Julia Child to our gastronomic world, has brought the elusive mousse and its many sub-forms within reach of us all. Historically, one kitchen worker with a strong arm could spend an arduous hour pounding the fish flesh and incorporating the cream that is now a job of a matter of seconds. Not to mention shellfish butters, which are now available at the flip of a switch. And far better too, I believe, because the still-cold fish mixes better, and holds the delicate airy form far better than when worked over bowls of ice as we did only twenty years ago.

For persons with regular access to salmon, less is always better, and the simple grill from the banks of the Moisie River in old Quebec, with a caper sauce and lemon at the side, is the very essence of the fish. But when you've got time in the kitchen, without question my favorite is the braised fish, rich in mushrooms and wine, called the Burgundy Darne.

This presentation is bursting with the charm of southern France, where the Ardor River runs down from the Pyrenees to the Atlantic. No fussy preparations are required or permitted: just good fish and good wine and good mushrooms, seasoned and thrown into a braising pan for an hour or so. The fish comes out with its natural silver raiment burnished like old family silver, and painted in the somber tones of burgundy wine, a surprising bonus to the uninitiated.

This was the delight of the old cooks of Provence, and it continues to surprise and delight me. The cooked skin reveals a wonderful character, and the flesh is succulent. It serves straight up, like a rib roast, and you carve it straight down, with the magnificent reduced mushrooms and glazed onions all around.

One of the most reliable methods for showcasing the unique salmon flavor without the contrast of oils is poaching. The result is always sublime, and the serving options thereafter are manifold. One unspoken rule of thumb concerns the preparation of the court bouillon, or poaching liquid. This is considered the short, or *court*, method of preparing a foundation, or *fond*, for cooking, because neither meat nor bones nor fish parts are used in its preparation.

If a whole fish is to be poached, the court bouillon should be assembled ahead of time, allowing the herbs and vegetables to blend with the wine over a low heat, and then be cooled to receive the whole fish without fear of the skin bursting from sudden contact with hot water. The whole fish and the court bouillon are then brought to a bare simmer together until cooked.

On the other hand, when the application is for steaks or fillets the accepted practice is to bring the court bouillon combination to a solid boil, and then back down on the heat until a bare simmer is maintained, and to introduce the steaks at that point. The lesser thickness of the flesh allows a heating-through more quickly, and the chance of splitting is reduced.

Equipment is important here, whether dealing with the whole fish or steaks and fillets. By convention the range of fish poachers grade up in 4-inch increments of length. A nominal 20-inch poacher will hold an entire 4- to 6-pound fish, perhaps with the tail bent slightly. A headless-tailless fillet of an 8- to 9-pound fish will also fit the 20-inch poacher.

If one were to attempt to poach whole a 10- to 12-pound fish, which is about 38 inches in length, one reaches the maximum poacher size of 40 inches. At about this weight, the fish becomes extremely large in the girth, and won't easily fit in any poacher.

I always insist on a one-sided poacher basket, with a string at each end to lift it, so that the cooked fish can be tipped out gently with minimum disruption. A fish breaking apart after poaching is not always a calamity, but it is always an event.

I remember once a very large fish, 38 pounds, was sent down from the Moisie River Salmon Club. That fish was nearly 48 inches long and posed a heroic challenge. Camille Berman, an imperious restaurateur charged with the job of cooking that great fish, never batted an eye. He cut it clean in two pieces, drawing his knife about two feet from the tip of the nose, cooking the front half separately from the remainder.

A spectacular cry went up from the guests as the brilliant salmon, borne high by two waiters and frocked out in green and silver mayonnaise, was transported triumphantly into the buffet. If you were in on the secret, you could see the artful line of mayonnaise and aspic decorations that curled down the fish's side at the very spot where the two had been reunited on their way out to the table.

Once, my bride-to-be and I were fishing the Russian River in Sonoma County California. It was a steelhead river, and the winds were crisp and the sky was bleak as I drowned flies throughout the morning. But it all seemed worthwhile later that day in a cozy taverna with a jolly chef who offered the local hors d'oeuvres — smoked steelhead nuggets.

I use his recipe here with salmon, and it seems to draw up the salts and acid flavors of the soy and brown sugar marinade, and give back a new flavor after a long, cool smoking over alder or juniper shavings. This is a process well suited to the backyard chef, and underscores the versatility of salmon.

In the very old days at Magdalen College they would have a "crimped" salmon brought out after the intramural tennis matches. It was very much the expected après-match dish, and was doubtless the last remnant of some long-forgotten Oxford Don's view of how life should be lived intramurally. The cold fish was overlaid with a variety of dreadful sauces in the old days, but in the modern incarnation the Sauce Nantua, so popular with pike and other cold fish, also saves the salmon.

Crimped salmon cannot be for the masses. In one unguarded moment even Escoffier described it as ". . . a barbarous method, which stiffens and contracts the flesh of the fish." Years later, always the alert politician, the "Chef of Kings and King of Chefs" softened his opinion slightly and said, in response to a query as to why he continued to serve the dish if it was so repugnant, "It is very difficult to say, and opinions on the matter are divided. This, however, is certain . . . fish prepared in this way is greatly relished by many."

And so the sauce can make the difference. Salmon sauces are legion, of course, but the greatest ones are the simplest. They usually have a roux at their heart that is blended with milk, which becomes a béchamel, or blended with fish or chicken stock which becomes a velouté. The base sauce is then lifted to its individual identity by the addition of herbs, prepared butters or spices.

Because salmon is strong, bright and up front, it does not need a sauce for camouflage, but merely for contrast. In the days before refrigeration, fish such as the Dover sole were widely known for the vast array of complicated sauces that were served with them. These were thought necessary because of the uncertain provenance of these delicate fish, and were served more to obscure than to illuminate their sublime flavor.

Let us pray that salmon will always be with us. The promise of fish farming is that there will never be a shortage. And these very worthwhile market fish can be served with the same enthusiasm bestowed on the wild fish who spent their last moments blasting up the river. The 34-pound fish that you caught in Nova Scotia on a fly you designed and tied yourself should be offered as simply and with as much restraint as you can manage under the circumstances.

The beautiful 8-pound silver-sided wonder with brilliant red flesh that you bought at the market is likewise a treasure, and should be carried aloft on a flaming spit with a herald of trumpets as it enters your living room for the amusement of your joyful, applauding clan.

GRILLED WHOLE SALMON WITH PINEAPPLE

A fanfare of trumpets heralded the spit-cooked salmon in ancient times.
The modern fish stuffed with pineapple, laced closed, and grilled in the backyard is more succulent and more accessible.

1 whole salmon, dressed and scaled, head on
3 tablespoons olive oil
2 cups pineapple chunks (or lemon pulp)
Salt and freshly cracked pepper

2 tablespoons bouquet garni, crushed
3 dried bay leaves, crushed
6 bamboo or poultry skewers
Cotton string

For grilling, the salmon should be less than 4 inches thick at the thickest point, located just behind the gill plate. Heavier fish may be filleted and each side grilled separately, giving special attention to the open side.

After the fish is dressed and carefully scaled, wash the fish quickly in cold water, then pat dry with paper towels. Rub the olive oil all over the fish, the head, the interior of the cavity and the skin and tail. Open the cavity and spread the pineapple chunks, salt and pepper, bouquet garni and crushed bay leaves on the inside. Secure the flaps of the cavity with the skewers and lace up with the string.

Over a prepared fire with dark (not bright) coals, or a pre-heated gas or electric grill with a setting of medium, use a wire brush to scour the grilling surface, then brush the grill with cooking oil. For very big fish use an extra grill that can be lifted and turned, or a fish basket.

Scatter some fire aromatics if desired and locate the grill 6 inches above the heat source. Place the fish just below the center-line of the grill, close the lid and open the circulation ports. Cook for 15 minutes without turning.

Using a long spatula, run down the length of the underside of the fish, carefully loosening any stuck bits.

Carefully roll the fish over from the open side so as to preserve the stuffing. Some skin will stick but it is unimportant. Cover the grill and continue cooking for an additional 10 minutes or more, for a total time, combining both sides, of at least 10 minutes per inch of thickness. (*Recipe continued on page 18.*)

GRILLED WHOLE SALMON WITH PINEAPPLE (CONTINUED)

The fish is done when the flesh flakes away to the pressure of a sharp knife tip at the dorsal fin, or an internal reading of 140°F at the thickest part. Remove the fish carefully to a large serving platter, and carve the fish into 3-inch sections from the top half, head to tail. Remove the backbone and continue serving from the under half.

Smoked Sonoma Samplers

Small-scale smoking is fun. It fills the participants with delusions of the simple life, and their clothes with mesquite and juniper smoke. The backyard smokers are ideal for small jobs, and the freshness of the fish is very noticeable.

2 pounds salmon fillet chunks (1-inch cubes), boned and skinned

FOR THE SONOMA COUNTY BRINE:
⅓ cup brown sugar
¼ cup salt
2 cups soy sauce
1 cup water
½ teaspoon minced garlic
½ teaspoon pulped onion
½ teaspoon ground cayenne pepper
1 cup white wine

Mix all the brine ingredients in a large saucepan, and warm slightly to aid in the dissolving of the sugar and salt. Allow the brine to cool. In a clean glass pickle jar or crockery jug, pack the salmon cubes and immerse completely in the brine. Top off the crock with water if necessary, and weight the fish to avoid floating. Place the crock, covered with aluminum foil, in the refrigerator for 12 hours, stirring once or twice.

Remove the fish chunks and allow them to drain on a rack. When a slight pellicle or skin has formed, place the salmon in the smoker, add flavor chips, and smoke over very low heat for up to 12 hours. The salmon chunks are done when they flake to a knife point. Serve at room temperature with a mustard sauce. The fish will keep for a week or two if stored in an airtight container.

Broiled Salmon Steaks and Roquefort Tomatoes

Big broiler flavors such as cheese and tomato can only be balanced by a big fish, like thick salmon steaks,
with a slightly sharp marinade and a crumb coating that brings the flavors together.

4 salmon steaks
2 garlic cloves, minced
3 flat anchovies
2 teaspoons dried oregano
4 tablespoons Worcestershire sauce

8 tablespoons olive oil, divided
4 small tomatoes
1 cup cornbread crumbs
4 tablespoons crumbled Roquefort cheese

In a small bowl combine the garlic, anchovies, oregano, Worcestershire, and 4 tablespoons olive oil into a sauce, stir and allow to marinate for half an hour. Cut off and discard the top ⅓ of each tomato. With a sharp knife make deep cuts across the inside of the tomato meat, preserving the skin, but cutting so as to open the space slightly. Spoon 1 tablespoon of the sauce over the top of each tomato and set them aside.

In a blender process the cornbread to a fine crumb, add the cheese and blend briefly to combine.

In a large skillet heat 4 tablespoons of olive oil over medium-high heat, and sauté one side only of the salmon steaks for 5 minutes, pushing them around to avoid sticking. Remove the salmon and scant cooking oil remaining to four individual ovenproof serving dishes, placing each steak, cooked side up, in a separate dish. Spoon one tablespoon of the remaining anchovy sauce over the top of each. Place one tomato, open side up, inside the ring of each salmon steak.

In an oven preheated to 400°F broil the 4 dishes in the upper ⅓ of the oven for 10 minutes, and avoid burning.

Scatter ¼ of the cornbread and cheese mixture over each steak and tomato (especially on the tomatoes) and return to the broiler for an additional 5 minutes, or until the cheese melts. Center each hot dish on a cool plate for handling and serve.

Salmon Quiche

Quiche is transportable, transmutable, and consistently popular. A crisp, golden pastry makes the dish, and plays against the salmon's strengths.
Even in a room-temperature service all the elements are at their best.

1½ cups cooked salmon, flaked, boned and skinned
4 tablespoons thinly sliced shallots
2 tablespoons unsalted butter
2 tablespoons cream sherry
2 tablespoons finely chopped fresh dill
3 large eggs, slightly beaten
½ cup heavy cream
½ cup crème fraîche
2 tablespoons cream cheese (garlic-flavored optional)
¼ teaspoon grated fresh nutmeg
Salt and pepper
½ cup grated Swiss cheese

FOR THE QUICHE PASTRY:
1¾ cups all-purpose flour
1 teaspoon salt
8 tablespoons unsalted butter, chilled
2 tablespoons vegetable shortening
1 egg yolk
3 tablespoons ice water

To make the pastry: Blend the flour, salt, butter and vegetable shortening carefully, then add the egg yolk and enough of the water for the dough to form into a ball. Wrap in wax paper and refrigerate for two hours. Lightly oil the quiche pan, then roll out the dough into a sheet about ⅜-inch thick. Carefully cut and fit the dough to the pan, molding the edges with your fingers.

Trim off any excess and refrigerate the pan and pastry for 15 minutes.

Line the pastry shell with wax paper, and place dry beans or small weights inside to keep the pastry from rising in the center. In an oven preheated to 375°F bake the pastry for 10 minutes, then remove the wax paper and weights and cook for an additional 5 minutes. Remove

(Recipe continued on page 24.)

Salmon Quiche (continued)

the partially cooked pastry from the oven and allow it to cool on a rack.

In a small skillet sauté the shallots in the butter, but do not allow them to brown. To the sauté add the sherry, dill and salmon, and stir gently to preserve flake size.

In a large bowl combine the eggs, heavy cream, crème fraîche, cream cheese, nutmeg, salt and pepper. Into the same bowl carefully spoon the sauté mixture, and stir once. Pour the quiche mixture into the pastry shell, then sprinkle the Swiss cheese over the top.

In an oven preheated to 375°F bake the quiche uncovered for 35 to 40 minutes, until the pastry is golden brown and the top of the pie is firm. Slice immediately and serve.

BROILED SALMON WITH HOLLANDAISE

The most simple fish gets the biggest sauce, and the addition of the pan juices makes a bold hollandaise that stands almost by itself.

4 salmon fillets, individual serving size
2 tablespoons olive oil
Salt and pepper
3 tablespoons butter
½ teaspoon ground cayenne pepper (or paprika)
1 tablespoon lemon juice

FOR THE HOLLANDAISE:
1½ cups (3 sticks) butter
3 large egg yolks
2 tablespoons water
1 tablespoon lemon juice
1 to 2 tablespoons of pan drippings

Butter the bottom of a baking dish large enough to accommodate all the fillets in a single row. Rub the fillets, top and bottom, with the olive oil. Place the fillets, skin side down, in the baking dish. Salt and pepper the fillets lightly.

In a small bowl combine the butter, cayenne and lemon juice. Cut this mixture into thin bits and place on top of the fillets. Under a broiler preheated to 500°F place the fish near the top of the oven and broil without turning until the fillets take on a rich, dark color. Reduce the heat to 350°F and continue cooking for a total of 10 minutes. Remove the fish and keep warm. Reserve pan drippings to add to the hollandaise.

For the hollandaise, melt the butter, without allowing it to brown, and remove it to a small pouring bowl.

Stir the egg yolks and water together and whisk the mixture in a bain marie or double boiler over low heat until the mixture begins to thicken. Remove from the heat and allow the mixture to continue thickening as you whisk. Slowly pour the butter into the egg mixture, whisking as you go to allow the butter and egg to blend into an emulsion. Slowly add the lemon juice and the pan drippings from the fish and continue whisking, returning to the heat as needed to keep the mixture warm. Serve immediately.

Top each fillet with a dollop of hollandaise and sprinkle the parsley around.

Noisettes du Saumon Meunière with Fried Parsley

Steaks of salmon are very adaptable, and trimmed of their skin and boned they change form easily, and roll into this dish whose only visual character is the wonderful crisp meunière covering. A slight sauce of fried parsley in butter balances with the delicate asparagus and leaves a clean palate.

2 large salmon steaks, at least 1 inch thick
1 egg, slightly beaten
¼ cup olive oil
⅓ cup flour
Salt and freshly cracked black pepper
½ teaspoon cayenne pepper

6 tablespoons butter, divided
⅓ cup chopped fresh parsley
2 tablespoons lemon juice
4 thin slices of lemon for garnish
4 bamboo skewers, each 4 inches long

Skin the steaks. Separate the flanks of each steak into two separate pieces, discarding the center bone and any remaining smaller bones.

In a bowl mix the egg and olive oil. Immerse the four salmon pieces and allow them to marinate in the egg and oil mixture for 20 minutes.

Mix the flour, salt and black and cayenne peppers together. Lift each piece of salmon from the marinade and roll lightly in the dredge to coat all sides. Roll each salmon piece into a flat coil, beginning with the larger end, and carefully circle until the tip is reached. Pin the tip of the meat with a bamboo or poultry skewer that is long enough to pierce through the thickest end of the salmon noisette and out the other side.

In a small skillet, soften 4 tablespoons of butter, and over medium heat sauté the noisettes, basting as you go, and turning to achieve a uniform brown color overall. Repeat for all four noisettes, then remove to serving dishes.

Melt 2 tablespoons of butter in the same skillet over low heat and allow to reach a slightly brown color. Add the parsley all at once, and stirring quickly, coat the parsley with the butter and allow it to take on slight color.

Remove the skewers from the now-cooled noisettes. Before serving, spoon the lemon juice over them and garnish with the sliced lemon and fried parsley. (*See procedure on page 88.*)

Skewered Salmon Slivers

The open fire changes everything in fish cooking; salmon skewers are graced with a whiff of the great outdoors and cook dry, calling for a basting from the bright oil and herb marinade.

2½ pounds skinned salmon fillets
1 tablespoon fresh rosemary, chopped and crushed
2 tablespoons olive oil
½ cup lemon juice
1 clove garlic, crushed
¼ cup dry sherry

¼ teaspoon salt
¼ teaspoon freshly cracked black pepper
¼ teaspoon cayenne
12 small green and red pepper wedges
12 small onion wedges
12 bamboo skewers

Crush the rosemary in a mortar. In a small bowl combine the rosemary, olive oil, lemon juice, garlic, sherry, salt, pepper and cayenne. Cut the salmon fillets into 1-by 4-inch strips. (Cut the fillet strips from head to tail rather than across the mediastinal muscle that runs down the center of the fish).

Place the salmon strips in the lemon, oil and herb mixture and marinate for 1 hour in the refrigerator, turning several times.

Remove the salmon from the marinade and shake dry. Reserve the marinade. Mount each sliver of salmon lengthwise on a skewer, piercing the salmon two or three times, and alternate with wedges of onion or pepper or both through the skewer.

Over a prepared fire with dark coals, brush the grill quickly with cooking oil, and place it 6 inches over the heat. Arrange the skewers in parallel lines in the center of the grill. Cook for 10 minutes before turning, brushing with the marinade as the food shows color. Serve over a plate of rice.

Scottish Timbales of Kedgeree

When the tourists in the great house turn up for their morning kipper, they also expect kedgeree, served these days on great puffs of pastry. When the red flag of the British Raj brought home a curry sauce to go with the fish, salmon was transformed into an excuse for a second stirrup cup.

2 cups warm, cooked salmon — skinned, boned and flaked
1 package puff pastry dough, enough for 4 timbales
1 cup thinly sliced onions
2 tablespoons butter
2 cups cooked rice
3 hard-boiled eggs

FOR THE CURRY-VELOUTÉ SAUCE:
3 tablespoons flour
4 tablespoons butter
1 tablespoon curry powder
2 cups clam juice
1 teaspoon dry mustard (or Punjabi garam masala, optional)

Roll out the puff pastry dough on a lightly floured flat surface, and cut four 5-inch squares of dough. Drape each square over a 3-inch muffin ring. Lightly squeeze the pastry to conform loosely to the shape of the ring. Either trim the square edges, or allow them to festoon. Set the rings with the pastry on an ungreased baking sheet. Place in an oven preheated to 400°F for 10 minutes. Turn the pastry and ring over and allow it to bake for another 5 minutes. Remove and allow to cool. Carefully work the ring out from inside the timbale. Crush down any pastry that has puffed up in the center of the timbale.

On the stovetop, sauté the onions in the butter until soft. Remove the onions from the pan and stir them into the cooked rice. Shell and chop the eggs and set them aside for the moment.

The curry-velouté is made from a roux of flour and butter and curry powder cooked for 3 to 5 minutes over very low heat, then flooded with the clam juice, and whisked over low heat for 10 minutes until a smooth, thick sauce is achieved. A double curry provides more interest, so in this case when the velouté has thickened somewhat, add 1 teaspoon of dry mustard or garam masala, and whisk constantly until absorbed. Cook over

(*Recipe continued on page 32.*)

SCOTTISH TIMBALES OF KEDGEREE (CONTINUED)

low heat for an additional 5 minutes without boiling. Adjust the seasonings with salt and pepper.

Assemble the timbales on a serving platter. Place 1 to 2 tablespoons of the curry-velouté in the bottom of each timbale, followed by a serving of the rice. Add ½ cup of the warm salmon flakes, top with a share of the chopped hard boiled eggs, and follow with a generous topping of the curry-velouté sauce.

SALMON SOUFFLÉ

A splash of ice water helps whip stiffer egg whites, and builds a stronger platform for the rich salmon nuggets.
Peel back the aluminum collar after cooking and serve this soufflé with a Chardonnay and a green salad.

⅓ cup salmon (boned and skinned), cooked and flaked
3 tablespoons butter
3 tablespoons flour
1 cup hot milk
½ teaspoon salt
½ teaspoon white pepper

½ teaspoon cayenne pepper
4 egg yolks
1 tablespoon ice water
5 egg whites
Aluminum foil and cotton string

Butter an 8-inch soufflé dish on the inside, and wrap a 6-inch band of double-folded aluminum foil around to form a collar or upward extension of the dish. The collar should rise 3 inches above the lip of the soufflé dish, and can be secured with three wraps of cotton string tied in a knot.

In a saucepan melt the butter over medium heat, then slowly stir in the flour, scraping until all is incorporated, making a roux. Reduce heat to the lowest possible, and continue working the mixture with a wooden spoon, removing from the heat before browning occurs, and continuing off and on over low heat for 5 minutes.

Add the hot milk and whisk into the roux, simmering for 3 minutes to achieve a very thick sauce.

Remove from the heat, then add the salt and peppers and stir. Pour this sauce into a large, warmed crockery mixing bowl. Stir in the egg yolks one at a time. Finally, add the salmon flakes, gently blending them into the sauce base.

In a chilled mixing bowl (copper is best), add 1 tablespoon ice water, and then the egg whites. Beat the mixture to stiff peaks. Spoon 2 tablespoons of the egg whites into the salmon mixture and incorporate. Spoon the rest of the egg whites on top of the salmon mixture and carefully fold the two together.

Tip the mixture into the collared bowl. Place in a preheated 400°F oven, and immediately reduce the temperature to 375°F. Bake the soufflé for 30 to 45 minutes, or until it has puffed 1 or 2 inches above the aluminum collar and is nicely browned. Serve immediately.

Burgundy Darne of Salmon

Where the River Arno runs down to the Atlantic, the French have pulled up salmon for centuries. They cook them simply, with a brilliant outcome as the wine is taken up by the fish and mushrooms, and produces a luxurious skin whose color and flavor will be a welcome surprise to all newcomers.

4-pound darne (midsection) of salmon, bone in but
   scaled
6 tablespoons butter, divided
Salt and pepper
½ cup thinly sliced onions
1 garlic clove, crushed and chopped

6 tablespoons chopped fresh parsley, divided
1 teaspoon dried thyme
1 bay leaf, crushed
2 cups sliced mushrooms
1 to 3 cups Burgundy wine, divided
½ cup fish stock

Rub butter over the fish, and sprinkle with salt and pepper. Place the darne in a well-buttered casserole or oven-proof braising dish. Sprinkle over, under and around it the onion, garlic, 3 tablespoons of parsley, thyme and crushed bay leaf. Add the mushrooms around the sides. Pour the wine over all, to less than midway up the side, and then cover the darne loosely with a sheet of buttered aluminum foil.

In an oven preheated to 400°F cook the dish for 10 minutes per inch of thickness or longer, basting frequently. When done the fish will have reached an internal temperature of 140°F. Remove the aluminum foil, baste, and cook 10 minutes longer as the fish skin takes on a dark, variegated color. Add wine as necessary to keep the fish moist.

Remove the fish to a hot platter, and keep warm while the sauce is prepared.

Strain the cooking liquid through a fine sieve, add the fish stock and up to another cup of burgundy wine to make a total of 1½ cups. In a saucepan over high heat, reduce this to about 1 cup, then add 5 tablespoons butter, whisking to a rich, frothy, thick sauce. Adjust the seasonings with salt and pepper, and pour a few tablespoons of the sauce over the fish. Add the remaining parsley and pour the rest of the sauce into a sauce boat. Serve with the mushrooms, glazed pearl onions and additional parsley.

NEW ENGLAND INDEPENDENCE DAY SALMON

*Poached salmon was so much a part of our early national heritage that it hardly seemed remarkable to Longfellow
that the first fish of the year was eaten ceremoniously by one of the most respectable citizens,
John Endicott, who was " . . . a comforable man with dividends, and the first salmon, and the first green peas . . ."*

I salmon fillet (2 to 3 pounds), skin on and boned
3 tablespoons chopped green onions and tops
I tablespoon butter
2 cups dry white wine
½ cup clam juice
Green peas, freshly shelled
Cooked new potatoes, rolled in butter and parsley
Lemon and parsley for garnish
Salt and pepper

FOR THE JOHN ENDICOTT ONION–EGG SAUCE:
2 tablespoons butter
½ cup thinly sliced onions
2 tablespoons flour
I cup reduced poaching liquid
¼ cup heavy cream
2 soft-boiled eggs

Scale the skin of the fillet, rinse, wipe dry and set aside. (Alternately, the fillet may be skinned and divided into serving pieces before cooking.) Sprinkle the chopped green onions and tops in a buttered baking pan just barely large enough to accommodate the fillet.

Rub the fillet with I tablespoon of butter. Salt and pepper the fillet and lay it skin side down over the green onions in the baking pan. Add the wine, clam juice, and enough water to bring the level almost to the top of the fillet. On top of the stove over medium heat bring the liquid to a simmer. Cover with aluminum foil, and remove to the lower half of a preheated 350°F oven. Cook at a bare simmer for 12 to 15 minutes. When the meat flakes easily to the tip of a knife it is done.

Arrange the fillet on a serving platter and cover to keep warm. Strain the poaching liquid and in a large saucepan over high heat reduce to I cup.

(*Recipe continued on page 38.*)

New England Independence Day Salmon (continued)

For the sauce: In a small sauté pan heat the butter and soften the onions without browning. Add the flour and stir constantly to make a roux. Add the reduced poaching liquid and whisk constantly until the sauce thickens. Remove from the heat and add the cream, whisking until it is thoroughly incorporated and the sauce has body. Shell the eggs, and crush them coarsely with the back of a fork. Blend the eggs carefully into the sauce. Salt and pepper to taste.

Garnish the platter with the new potatoes, rolled in parsley and butter, and the boiled fresh green peas. Serve the fillet whole or in slices, with some sauce on top. Pass the remaining sauce in a sauce boat.

CRIMPED SALMON MAGDALEN WITH SAUCE NANTUA

At Oxford, and certainly at Magdalen College there, the students had many odd traditions. And crimped salmon, being one of the oddest, was served as a buffet after intramural tennis. For this unique presentation to make the short list of modern gastronomy it needed a rescue. A very bright Sauce Nantua, perhaps even with a suggestion of pepper, showcases the sturdy underlying salmon and makes a brilliant display.

1 whole salmon, 4 to 6 pounds
1 cup white wine
Water to cover

6 tablespoons salt
2 cups Sauce Nantua (*see recipe on page 78*)
20-inch fish poacher

Place the salmon on a large cutting board and carefully scale and dress the fish. Rinse and wipe dry. With the fish on its side, using a large sharp knife make diagonal gashes across the skin of the fish every two inches from gill plate to tail fin. The gashes should be deep (to the center of the fish) and long (from the dorsal line to the open cavity). Then reverse the fish and repeat the process.

Place the salmon in a poacher of sufficient size to allow the fish to rest at full length. Cover with cold water to which has been added 1 cup of white wine. Place the entire assembly — fish, water and wine and poacher — in the freezer for one hour.

Remove the poacher from the freezer and discard the water and wine. Add enough fresh water at room temperature to reach the fish's back. Add 6 tablespoons salt to the water. Place the poacher over two burners and quickly bring to a boil. Reduce the temperature immediately to a simmer, and watch the fish, uncovered, until it is done.

The fish is done when the dorsal fin is loose to the touch, or when an internal temperature of 145°F is reached. It is critical to remove the fish quickly at this point, allow it to dry briefly, wipe clean, and remove the skin and fins. Serve with the Sauce Nantua in a sauce boat.

"OLD TWEED ON THE RIVER"

"No salmon in the English rivers, dear boy! The last fish caught in the Thames was at Taplow. 1824, as I recall. Pollution and what not, you know. You're quite right to look to Scotland!"

The Tourist smiled, grateful for the information. Across the large, paneled room other guests were gathering for an evening drink. Portraits of ancient highland chieftains glowered down from the walls. A few yew logs smoldered in the stone fireplace as the footman passed a note to Lord Tweed.

His Lordship read the note at a glance, folded it quickly into the pocket of his dinner jacket, and resumed his conversation. "So don't be intimidated by all this history." He waved his hand toward the vaulted stone ceiling, and out toward the lead-mullioned windows that gave a glimpse of the sun falling across the lough. "Americans always resist history. They want a new answer to every old challenge. Trust me," said Lord Tweed as he put one hand on the Tourist's shoulder, "the old ways are the best!"

Just then the butler burst through the doors from the pantry, holding head-high an immense silver platter. At its center, glazed and gleaming, a thirty-pound salmon cast a baleful eye of radish and olive on the assembled guests, reproaching the lot of them as it floated by. The murmurs around the room turned to a chorus of polite applause, and the guests drifted into the wake of the fish, following it into the great dining room.

Lord Tweed and the Tourist lingered in the drawing room. "See here," His Lordship said, tugging on the visitor's sleeve, "I don't often do this, but you've been here the entire week without a fish. Dreadful unlucky. And you seem a likely chap. Please take this," he said, as he placed a single salmon hook, dressed like an angry black fly, wrapped in gold tinsel with bristling feather wings into the Tourist's hand. "It's a Jock Scott. It's seen one hundred years on this river, and it'll see you through tomorrow."

The Tourist protested. His Grace stood firm. The Tourist offered to pay. His Lordship closed his eyes with a shiver of protest at the very mention of lucre.

"I'll have old Pincher assigned to you in the morning," His Lordship said. "Tell him I said you were to catch a fish at Parson's Pool, and I have given you my grandfather's last Jock Scott to do it with!"

And so it went for the rest of the evening. The guests were all tourists in one form or another, temporary British gentlemen out for a week of the gilded sporting life. Lord Tweed bobbed and weaved his way around the room. A story here, a family anecdote there, a snap of his fingers for more drinks. The only awkward moment came with the two foreign guests, but when it developed that they knew all about single-malt scotch Lord Tweed was again in his element and the evening drifted into twilight and cigars over port, contemplating the rush of wild fish up the river.

The salmon fly-fishing rush really only started in the middle of the nineteenth century, when sporting Englishmen came North, raising the rents along every salmon river, and driving out the native Scots' "torch and spear" fishing brigade.

This "gentle epidemical mania for salmon fishing," as the local parson described it, caught up all in its wake. The poet Sir Walter Scott, when frustrated with hook and line, was known to participate in clandestine episodes of the madly diverting torchlight spearing.

By 1880 every rod on the popular Lyon River, in West Perthshire, was a paying guest who had booked months in advance for the privilege of unlimbering his gut lines and casting the early flies tied by a shoemaker named John Younger.

Together with the lure of the fish there was, for the English, a fascination with the etiquette of flies and the protocol of presentation. The British and European fly patterns had a brief evolution, and then froze in a rigid stylized orthodoxy, like Pleistocene bugs in amber, that has never changed to the present.

There was the Jock Scott and the Hairy Mary, and a half-dozen other fanciful names — including the Green Highlander, the Darbee Spate Fly, and the Dusty Miller — whose origins are all but lost to us today, but whose relevance is reasserted after every successful cast. They were tied, or "dressed," according to a very strict legend using all of the exotic natural materials available. Great business enterprises grew up, providing the sporting gents with an endless supply of wetable-feather insects.

But no pattern was perfect, and the salmon continued to provoke and confound. Their annual return to the river being dedicated to but a single purpose — procreation — they weren't much interested in food. That's why no one quite knew what to offer or how to provoke a strike.

Joseph Pulitzer, the publisher of the St. Louis newspaper and founder of the journalism prize that bears his name, is given credit for creating the now very popular "Rusty Rat" pattern. His luck came after a hard day of fishing that saw his traditional fly, a Black Rat, take a shredding on the rocks and trees that exposed the orange body wrapping underneath. His gillie suggested a change, but Pulitzer cast one more time, and hooked and landed a 41-pound salmon in the Brandy Brook waters of New Brunswick in 1949. The publisher gave all credit to the newly designed fly, which he dubbed "a rusty rat."

Down by the lough, however, and by the light of the full moon, the yeomen and practical-minded squires still netted, and fished with hooks festooned with bright red salmon roe. No one yet knows quite why salmon take a hook in the first place, but poachers know that fish eggs, bright red jewels from the hen salmon's nest, are always successful. Some theorize a combination of the right atmospheric pressure and the appropriate oxygen content of the water provoke strikes. Others put it down to the irritable, territorial nature of the fish, fighting their way up against terrific current forces, grateful for a moment's rest in a still pool among the turbulence.

But that doesn't stop tourists all over the fishing world from buying the local flies, whether in New Brunswick or Norway. Over and over again, even the most scientific and sophisticated of anglers have subscribed to the theory that these patterns are river specific. When the sport of fishing for salmon with wet flies spread to America, the British fly patterns were adapted so as to be made with indigenous materials, such as bear and moose. New patterns began to emerge — one for high water, one for low water, one for early in the morning and one for late in the day, until there was an accepted canon of flies for each and every salmon river in North America.

The Quebec and Nova Scotia rivers have always been fountains of salmon. When Iver Adams and his stalwart mates "discovered" the Moisie River in Quebec, it was a remote wilderness camp beyond the ends of the earth. The club he founded spent the next hundred years liberating the river from the indigenous netters and commercial fishermen. It is argued, by the members of that exclusive club, that rivers like the Moisie had their youth greatly extended by the aristocratic fishing clubs. It must be said that for all their exclusivity, the club members certainly contributed to the community, and got the river into a more or less healthy state well in advance of the rise of conservationism as a national or even a sporting ethic.

Originally the club had eight or nine members who could knock off for a few weeks in the summer, and didn't mind the arduous trek to the camp. To help with the upkeep, however, they let it be known that they were looking for the "right sort of chap" to fill out the membership list. Little did they expect when they offered "a rod" to the fashionable Lapsley family of Pomfret, Connecticut, that the all male ethos of the fishing at the Moisie River Salmon Club was about to change forever.

On that first morning the Montagnais Indians sitting on the bank were too reserved to giggle. The Quebeçois gaffers, Pere Pacquet and Ardias Mercier, clamped sternly on their unlit pipes as they stood beside their waiting canoes. Across the river shingle, marching straight up to them, came the impossibly fashionable twin sisters known as Mrs. A.B. Lapsley and Mrs. P.G. Birkenhead.

All irreverent sniggering stopped almost immediately. The sisters were tall and svelte and dressed to the nines in the buff whipcords and snug cloche hats that made the flappers famous back home. In spite of their carefully turned chamois gloves the women caught 490 salmon between them during the next three weeks. They fished 15-foot rods, and were the delight of guests and camp regulars. They are recorded in the club books as the number-one and number-two anglers for the year 1926.

The art and practice of casting for salmon is thoughtful work. Sometimes an hour of repetitive blind casting across a known lie at a single pool, changing hook size or fly pattern or both several times, is necessary. And the magnificent rivers of western Canada offered Pacific salmon such as the King that were energetic enough to take a floating dry fly.

Sport fishing for salmon worldwide began to take on the theatrical drama of a tiger hunt from shikarries mounted on elephants. Dandys showed up in Scotland, Ireland, Nova Scotia or British Columbia, dressed themselves in the local rag, twisted down a small fortune, then pretended to be great sporting gentlemen, all in the name of the mighty silver fish — the salmon.

The next morning Pincher looked at his old pocket watch. It was 11:00 AM and the bus would soon be pulling up to the great house, unloading one gaggle of new gentlemen tourists, and collecting another. He had now watched this particular Tourist for three hours. The Jock Scott had hit the tree, hit the rock, and even hit a bush on the far bank. Parson's Pool had been thoroughly explored, but no fish had risen.

After the next cast and retrieve Pincher stepped briskly up beside his charge, and gently took the rod into his own hands. "I'll have a look at this fly," he said. "May have caught a leaf on it."

With his back to the Tourist, old Pincher worked furiously with his fingers, reaching into the great baggy pockets of his old tweed jacket twice, and tied the Tourist's bait with a flurry of stiff fingers that were embarked on an urgent mission.

"I'll have a go this time," Pincher said, "just for luck!" And with that the gillie stepped into the cast and with a quick underhand roll sent the hook and all sailing into the middle of Parson's Pool where it dropped with a heavy splash. The hook sank quickly and went straight to the bottom.

Pincher straightened his back, tugged once or twice on the line with his free hand, and passed the rod to the Tourist. "Just about there, sir," he said as he reached over and yanked the line once more. "Now you hold steady, and count to five when you feel him taking the slack. Then break the back of it good and proper, and we'll finally have him after all this!"

Just then the line went tight with the power of a big salmon at the other end. The line cut across the surface of the water as the Tourist counted to five, and set the hook. Pincher let out a shriek, and the fight was on.

Together they reeled and back-walked. They lost the net when someone kicked it in the river. Pincher put his arms around the Tourist and with four hands they reeled and kept the rod tip aloft. Eventually the exhausted fish was dragged up on the bank.

It was a big fish, maybe 24 pounds. The Tourist gripped the tail with both hands, knuckles turning white like a weight lifter, and raised the tail to his chin. Pincher took a few photographs.

Smiling out from the corner of the salmon's locked jaw was the new Jock Scott, carefully wrapped in a handful of bright red salmon eggs that hung down like grapes on a vine.

"Trust me," said Pincher as he snipped off the fly, and wiped away the roe. "The old ways are the best!"

Foil Boats in the Sunset

The curling wisps of flavored smoke from the backyard grill reach over the gunnels of the foil boat, and bathe the fish in a wood-smoke accent that no oven can match. Slide the cooked fillets onto a plate for serving, and offer a spoonful of basmati rice to catch the cooking juices.

4 salmon steaks, approximately 1½ inches thick, bone in
½ cup thinly sliced scallions
2 tablespoons butter
½ teaspoon dried thyme, crushed

4 lemon slices, paper thin
4 tablespoons dry white wine
Salt and pepper
Heavy-duty aluminum foil

Make a "boat" for each salmon steak using a double thickness of foil. The boats should be slightly larger than the steaks and about 2 inches tall. Do not close the top of the boats.

Into each boat sprinkle an equal portion of the scallions. Salt and pepper the steaks and place on top of the scallions. Divide the butter into thin slices and place equally on top of each steak. Sprinkle the thyme evenly among the steaks, and then place one lemon slice directly in the center of each steak. Gently pour 1 tablespoon of wine around the inside edge of each boat.

Over a fairly hot and smoking grill, place all the boats on the grill at one time, allowing the smoke to curl through the open boats and influence the steaks. Close the lid on the grill and allow to cook rapidly for about 10 minutes.

Each boat may be placed on individual serving plates, or may be disassembled by an ambitious host.

COLD SALMON WARRIOR IN CUCUMBER ARMOR

Poached salmon is the purest presentation of the great fish's qualities. And in a cold buffet the addition of green mayonnaise secures the translucent slices of cucumber, yet still allows the salmon's flavor to be very much in front.

1 whole salmon (4 to 6 pounds), dressed and scaled
1 stuffed olive
2 cups green mayonnaise (*see recipe on page* 77)
3 cucumbers, sliced in very thin rounds and chilled
Lemon and radicchio for garnish

FOR THE COURT BOUILLON:
1 cup thinly sliced onions
2 tablespoons olive oil
8 cups dry white wine
2 tablespoons bouquet garni
2 bay leaves
¼ teaspoon freshly cracked pepper
6 cups water

First make the court bouillon by combining the onions and olive oil in a small saucepan and softening the onions for 5 minutes without browning. In a 20-inch fish poacher combine the softened onions, wine, bouquet garni, bay leaves, pepper and 1 cup of water and bring to a simmer for 10 minutes. Allow the court bouillon to cool in the poacher.

Place the whole fish in a natural swimming position on a tray that fits in the poacher, and lower it into the court bouillon. Add water to bring the level to the top of the fish.

Bring the fish and poaching liquid quickly to a simmer, and then reduce the heat to maintain a simmer for about 30 minutes. The fish should cook for a period of time equal to 10 minutes per inch of thickness of the fish, measured just behind the gills. (In a 4- to 6-pound fish the thickness will be about 3 inches, and the cooking time will be 30 minutes.) The fish is done when the dorsal fin is pliable at its base, or the skin flakes away from the dorsal fin easily to the touch of a knife.

Remove the fish, and allow it to drain briefly. Place the salmon on a serving platter, lying on one side. (*Recipe continued on page 52.*)

Straighten the tail if necessary, and allow it to cool on its side. Remove the eye and replace with a stuffed olive.

Using a small knife, cut a line in the skin from back to belly just behind the gill plate, and another one at the other end just before the tail. Using a dull spoon and a knife blade, remove all the skin of the fish from the exposed side between these two cuts.

Coat the top surface of the fish with the green mayonnaise. Beginning at the tail, lay the cucumber slices like paving tiles across the fish until you reach the head. Decorate the head with mayonnaise (or aspic if you wish) and serve the fish on the platter. If the diners get through the top half, remove the backbone by severing it at the head and tail and lifting it out. Coat the remaining surface with more mayonnaise, and cucumbers if you like, and take it back for another round.

Salmon Terrine

Fish terrines soar on a very light forcemeat, with all ingredients and utensils chilled beforehand. Small fillets of fish or bits of shrimp can be introduced to give a different focus to this dish, but success lies with an airy, cold, whipped medium of fish and egg white.

3 cups of salmon fillet chunks, skinned and boned
6 tablespoons heavy cream (or crème fraîche)
6 eggs
½ teaspoon ground cayenne pepper
½ teaspoon each salt and pepper

½ cup celery, thinly sliced on the bias
3 cups shelled green peas
1 cup finely chopped parsley
⅓ cup finely chopped chives
Green mayonnaise (*see recipe on page* 77)

Refrigerate all ingredients. Place the chunks of salmon in a processor bowl and whir briefly for 30 seconds. Add half the cream, 3 eggs, cayenne, salt and pepper in a bowl and mix thoroughly. Then add to the fish and process in short bursts for about 1 minute.

In a large saucepan bring 4 cups of water with 1 tablespoon of salt to a boil. Parboil the peas and celery for 4 minutes. Remove, drain and pat dry. In a processor bowl combine the drained peas, celery, parsley and chives, add some salt and pepper, and whir briefly for 30 seconds. Add the remaining 3 tablespoons of cream and continue to process for 30 seconds. Add the remaining 3 eggs and process for another 30 seconds, or until all ingredients have formed a smooth mousse.

Butter the inside of a 6-cup terrine. If the terrine is to be decanted before serving, line the sides and bottom with buttered wax paper cut to fit. Spoon half of the salmon mixture evenly across the bottom. Cover this with the pea mousse, spooning into the corners to avoid air pockets. Finish with the remaining salmon. Cover with buttered wax paper or aluminum foil, then the terrine lid. Place the terrine in a bain marie, or an open roasting pan with 1 inch of boiling water.

In an oven preheated to 350°F cook for about 1 hour. The terrine is done when it reaches an internal temperature of 145°F. Remove and allow to cool for 1 hour. Refrigerate overnight before serving with green mayonnaise to taste.

Salmon Fillets Stuffed with Shrimp Mousse

Mousse is always a balance of flavors, and one has scope for expression in the assembly and seasoning.
The raw shrimp protein will bind the rice and flavors during cooking, and the addition of an anchovy will up the fish flavor scale.
In the other direction, the addition of crumbled nuts favors the somber tones.

6 salmon fillets (2 to 3 pounds total), boned and
   skinned
¼ cup finely diced onions
2 garlic cloves, crushed and minced
4 tablespoons peanut oil, divided
1 cup uncooked brown basmati rice
3 flat anchovy fillets
2½ cups vegetable stock

1 tablespoon potato starch
¼ teaspoon each salt and pepper
2 egg whites
2 cups raw shrimp, peeled
½ cup grated sharp white cheese
2 cups fine French bread crumbs, no crust
2 tablespoons butter
⅓ cup dry sherry

In a pot large enough for 3 cups of cooked rice, soften the onions and garlic in 2 tablespoons of peanut oil over low heat for 5 minutes without browning. Add the rice, anchovies, stock, potato starch, salt and pepper and simmer covered for 30 minutes, stirring regularly until the rice is tender, adding more liquid if necessary to keep moist.

Beat the egg whites in a chilled bowl (copper is best) with 1 tablespoon ice water, until they form soft peaks.

In a processor blend the shrimp, egg whites, and grated cheese for 10 seconds until thoroughly blended. Transfer to a mixing bowl.

Fold the rice mixture carefully into the shrimp mixture. Add up to 2 cups of the bread crumbs — enough to hold form as patties. Using ¾ cup of this mixture for each, form six rectangular patties (about 3 x 4 inches long and ¾ of an inch thick). Place on an oiled baking sheet and refrigerate for 30 minutes.

(*Recipe continued on page 56.*)

Salmon Fillets Stuffed with Shrimp Mousse (continued)

The skinned salmon fillets should be cut in half along the long axis of the fish to create fillets that are about 2½ x 4 inches long and 1 inch thick. On a cutting board, lay the flat side of a cleaver against each fillet and tap with a kitchen hammer to flatten each fillet, forming fillets about 7 inches long and 4 inches wide, slightly wider and 1 to 2 inches longer than the rice/shrimp patties.

Salt and pepper the salmon, then wrap one salmon fillet around each rice/shrimp patty, tucking the ends underneath. Place all the stuffed fillets in a buttered roasting pan. Add the butter, remaining peanut oil and sherry to the pan. Place a sliver of butter on top of each fillet. Cover each salmon fillet with a square of aluminum foil and cook in an oven preheated to 400°F for 20 minutes, basting regularly. (*See procedure on page 92.*)

Sailor's Stove-top Poach with Tartar Sauce

This was a favorite for one-handed cooks on Puget Sound trawlers dragging for coho,
and was popular when Jake Hershey's "Bluebonnet" sailed in the Southern Ocean Racing Circuit.

8 salmon steaks (each about 1 inch thick)
Water to cover
4 tablespoons white vinegar

FOR THE TARTAR SAUCE:
2 cups green mayonnaise (*recipe on page* 77), or prepared mayonnaise
2 hard-boiled eggs, shelled and diced fine
2 tablespoons prepared mustard
1 sour dill pickle, diced fine
3 tablespoons capers, drained and diced
Salt and pepper

Fill a large saucepan with 2 inches of water and the vinegar. Bring the water to a boil, then reduce the heat to a simmer.

Add the salmon steaks all at once (space permitting), and cook for about 8 minutes. The steaks are done when the skin flakes away from the meat at the touch of a knife tip. Remove the steaks with a spatula and allow to dry on a rack while you prepare the sauce.

In a large mixing bowl combine the green mayonnaise, hard-boiled eggs, mustard, pickle and capers and combine thoroughly with a fork or a small potato masher. Add salt and pepper to taste. Serve this sauce with the poached fish.

Coulibiac Russe

Happy Russian serfs left nothing to waste and ate their salmon and hearty pastry with gusto.
But in the belle époque of Europe this dish had a renaissance, a name change, and an elevation of status to "trophy food."
The savory velouté designed by Escoffier lends a subtlety and transition to the flavors.

4 cups cooked salmon (skinned and boned)
½ cup chopped dill, divided
Salt and pepper
4 tablespoons butter, divided
1 tablespoon olive oil
2 cups thinly sliced onions, divided
¾ cup rice
1 cup beef consommé

½ teaspoon nutmeg
1 tablespoon minced garlic
1 cup thinly sliced mushrooms
2 hard-boiled eggs, coarsely chopped
1 cup fish velouté sauce *(see recipe on page 81)*
1 tablespoon chopped parsley
1½ pounds brioche dough *(see recipe on page 82)*
1 egg yolk beaten with a little milk for glazing

Flake the salmon into spoon-sized pieces and mix with ¼ cup dill. Salt and pepper to taste. Refrigerate this mixture.

In 2 tablespoons of butter and the olive oil, sauté 1 cup of the onions for 5 minutes without browning. Add the rice and stir constantly over low heat for 3 minutes, or until the grains are glazed. Add the consommé and nutmeg. Salt to taste. Cover and simmer until the rice is soft. Turn the rice out onto a baking sheet, and allow to cool.

Sauté the rest of the onions and the garlic in 2 tablespoons of butter. Add the mushrooms and allow the mixture to take on a slight color. Turn out to cool on a plate.

In a large bowl combine the mushrooms, the eggs, the velouté sauce, parsley and remaining dill. Check for seasoning.

Roll out half of the brioche dough into a 12- x 8-inch rectangle by ¼-inch thick. Place this dough on an oiled baking sheet. Using half of the rice mixture, form a thin rectangle from the center of the dough that is 1 inch smaller than the brioche around the edges.

(Recipe continued on page 60.)

Coulibiac Russe (continued)

Spoon half of the salmon flakes into a layer over the rice, then another layer of the rice, and a final layer of salmon, pressing down each layer gently. Cover the final layer with the mushroom, egg and velouté mixture.

To form a pastry lid, roll out the remaining dough into a 18- x 10-inch rectangle by ¼-inch thick. Brush the edges of the dough base with the egg and milk mixture, and gently lower the lid into place. Seal the edges firmly together with the back of a fork. Trim off any excess pastry and roll out to create Russian motifs of vines and leaves and figs. Cut and trim a vent hole in the center of the pastry lid and insert a foil funnel. Brush the lid of the case with egg and milk and apply decorations.

Brush the entire top of the coulibiac once more with egg and milk and bake in an oven preheated to 400°F for 40 minutes, or until the crust is golden brown. Use a thin strip of aluminum foil over the decorations to prevent browning if necessary. *(See procedure on page 90.)*

Smoked Salmon Omelettes

Always warm the salmon in butter; the omelette cooks quicker through the middle and leaves the edges soft.
Gravlax can be substituted for the smoked salmon.

INGREDIENTS PER EACH OMELETTE:
⅓ cup smoked salmon, cut in thin slivers
2 tablespoons butter
2 tablespoons chopped parsley

2 large eggs
1 teaspoon cold water
Salt and pepper

In a skillet over low heat sauté all the salmon slivers and parsley needed per omelette in butter until they are all warm and well coated. Remove and set aside.

Mix the eggs for one omelette in a separate small bowl with a teaspoon of water and salt and pepper. Stir briefly to break the yolks.

In an omelette pan over high heat melt 2 tablespoons of butter. As the foam subsides pour in the egg mixture, and shake the pan to even out the cooking of the eggs. Allow the eggs to cook for a few seconds, and then quickly add a portion of the smoked salmon mixture, spread in a line across the lower third of the eggs.

With a strong upward and backward hand motion repeatedly roll the omelette's near edge over the filling, using a spatula to help with the rolling if necessary. When the roll is complete allow the omelette to cook for a minute longer until the uncooked edges begin to curl slightly. Turn the omelette onto a serving plate and proceed for each additional omelette.

Swedish Gravlax

Curing fish with salt and sugar is not reserved to wizened old smokehouse proprietors glaring out from their dark shanties along the banks of the fjord. This application avoids preservatives, comes fresh from the ocean, and slices thin. No more than a mere suggestion of the bright horseradish mustard will suffice.

2½ pounds fresh salmon (about 6 inches of centercut, top and bottom), skin on
¼ cup salt
⅓ cup brown sugar (or white sugar)

2 teaspoons freshly cracked pepper
2 cups coarsely chopped fresh dill
Horseradish mustard (*see recipe on page* 77)

Scale the skin and rub the fish clean with a moist towel. Fillet out both sides of the centercut, leaving the bones behind, and run your finger along the meat side of each fillet to identify and complete the small bone removal with kitchen pliers.

Combine the salt, sugar, and pepper in a bowl and mix thoroughly. In a large glass roasting dish or earthenware platter, place the fillets skin side down and side by side. Rub the surfaces with half of the salt mixture. Spread the fresh dill thickly over the exposed surface of one fillet, and then cover, meat side down, with the other fillet. Rub the remaining salt mixture over the skin sides of the fillets.

Tightly cover the fillets and the glass dish with aluminum foil so there are no air holes. Place a light weight on top of the fillets, and refrigerate for 48 hours. After the first 4 hours the fluid should be poured off the gravlax, and then resealed and refrigerated.

To serve, position the fillet skin side down, and cut paper thin slices on a bias, leaving the skin behind. Serve each morsel on thin slices of rye bread, as with smoked salmon, and accompany with horseradish mustard sauce. (*See procedure on page 86.*)

Batter-dipped Salmon Chops with Cabbage

North of Chicago there was once a windy roadside diner that specialized in chops of all kinds. They even offered a salmon cut like a chop, which is remembered fondly, while everything else about the restaurant is long gone from place and memory.

2 salmon steaks (each about 1½ inches thick), skinned and boned
6 cups cabbage, washed and cut in ¼-inch strips
2 tablespoons fennel seeds, slightly crushed
2 tablespoons canola oil
2 tablespoons butter

FOR THE SAUCE (OPTIONAL):
6 tablespoons butter, divided
2 tablespoons vinegar
2 tablespoons heavy cream
Salt and freshly ground black pepper

FOR THE DREDGE:
2 slices bacon, cut in ¼-inch strips
½ cup milk
½ teaspoon thyme
1 egg, slightly beaten
½ cup fresh bread crumbs
2 tablespoons chopped parsley
Salt and freshly ground black pepper

Bring 2 quarts of salted water to a boil, and parboil the cabbage strips for 2 minutes, retaining some crispness. Drain, cool and toss with the crushed fennel seeds.

Make a dredge by cooking the bacon strips in a skillet for 3 minutes over medium heat until soft. Add the milk and thyme, and stir for 1 minute. In a processor purée this mixture until smooth. Then add the egg, bread crumbs, parsley and salt and pepper and blend for another 2 minutes and reserve.

With a sharp knife separate each meaty half of the salmon steaks from the spinal bone in the center. Trim each piece in the shape of a "chop" and flatten slightly with your hand, or the flat side of a cleaver.

Heat the oil and butter in a skillet large enough to accommodate the four chops. Dip each chop in the dredge on both sides and fry for 5 minutes per side over medium-high heat until brown. Remove the chops and (*Recipe continued on page 66.*)

Batter-dipped Salmon Chops with Cabbage (continued)

keep warm. Toss the drained cabbage and fennel in the same skillet over low heat for 1 minute. Remove the cabbage and pan drippings to serving plates and place the chops on top of the cabbage.

If sauce is desired, melt 4 tablespoons butter in a small skillet until it begins to turn dark. Remove the skillet from the heat and whisk in the vinegar. Return the skillet to low heat, add 2 tablespoons butter and the cream and continue whisking over very low heat until it thickens. Add salt and pepper and pour over the chops and cabbage.

Cold Salmon Salad with Avocado

Just like choosing a salmon hook, when it comes to salads the dressing is everything. Since the fish will be bold, very fresh herbs such as rosemary can be crushed into the dressing without too much surprise.

2 cups cooked salmon, boned, skinned and flaked
½ cup mayonnaise
½ cup sour cream
3 tablespoons finely chopped green onions
¼ cup minced celery root

½ cup chopped cilantro leaves
1 teaspoon Tabasco sauce
Salt and pepper to taste
2 avocados, skinned, seeded and halved lengthwise

Combine the mayonnaise, sour cream, green onions, celery, cilantro, Tabasco, salt and pepper in a mixing bowl ahead of time and refrigerate until ready to serve.

Arrange the four avocado halves as open boats, each on a leaf of lettuce. Carefully fold the salmon flakes into the dressing, mixing gently until the fish is coated.

Spoon the mixture into the avocado halves. Sprinkle with freshly ground black pepper and serve with lemon wedges.

MOISIE RIVER GRILL WITH CAPER SAUCE

When the salmon fishermen packed their gear for a few weeks in the wilds of Old Quebec, they often brought an extra jar of capers, nestled safely in a pair of heavy socks, so they wouldn't miss the great treat of a rich caper sauce on a slab of salmon fillet.

1 salmon fillet (about 2 to 3 pounds), skin on and
  boned
2 tablespoons olive oil
1 tablespoon salt
1 tablespoon freshly cracked black pepper
2 tablespoons melted butter for brushing (or olive oil)

FOR THE CAPER SAUCE:
2 tablespoons butter
2 tablespoons flour
2 cups fish stock (or clam juice)
1 teaspoon crushed green peppercorns
6 tablespoons large Italian or Greek capers with brine

For the caper sauce: In a sauté pan combine the butter and flour over very low heat, stirring constantly. Do not allow the roux to brown. When the bubbles in the butter are tiny and uniform, add the stock slowly, whisking constantly until the roux thickens, about 5 minutes. Add the green peppercorns during this stage and continue stirring.

Remove from the heat and add the capers and brine, crushing the berries with the back of a large spoon to release their flavor. Return to low heat and stir, incorporating the contents. Adjust for taste with salt and pepper.

Scale and rinse the fillet, and allow it to drip dry. Rub olive oil over the meat and skin and remove any remaining bones. Salt and pepper the fish.

Over a prepared fire with dark (not bright) coals, or an electric or gas grill preheated and set to medium, add any aromatic bits such as wood chips or broken bay leaves as desired. Place the fillet, skin side up, for a brief smoking of about 8 minutes, covered.

Using a long spatula, run down the length of the underside of the fillet, carefully loosening any stuck meat. Carefully roll the fillet over. Some meat will stick but it is unimportant. Baste the flesh side with the butter, cover the grill and continue cooking for 10 minutes or more, basting as necessary. The fish is done when the flesh flakes away to the pressure of a sharp knife tip at the intersection between skin and meat, or at an internal reading of 140°F at the thickest part.

Remove the fillet to a cutting board and serve each portion by carving vertical sections, at least 4 inches wide, skin and all, and top each with the caper sauce.

Quenelles of Salmon on Pasta with Tomato Bisque

These floating puffs of salmon essence can only be made with a food processor, whose contribution to cooking in America is only slightly less portentious than that of Julia Child herself. The creamy tomato bisque, à la Child, moistens the quenelles and complements the al dente fettuccine.

2 cups raw salmon chunks (from a 1½-pound fillet,
　skinned and boned)
1 egg
1 teaspoon salt
1 teaspoon freshly cracked pepper
¼ teaspoon ground nutmeg
2 tablespoons minced fresh chives

½ cup heavy cream
½ cup French bread crumbs
1 tablespoon Cognac
2 cups tomato bisque (*see recipe on page 80*)
¼ cup dry sherry
2 cups spinach fettuccine, cooked
Parsley for garnish

Chill all ingredients thoroughly, as well as the bowl and blade of the food processor. Place the fish cubes in the processor bowl, add the egg, salt and pepper, nutmeg, chives and cream. Process this mixture using a dozen short pulses for a total of 30 seconds or more. Scrape down the sides and repeat with 6 more pulses.

Sprinkle in 6 tablespoons of the bread crumbs, add the cognac and process for 3 seconds. Now evaluate the mousse. If it is flaccid and shapeless it needs more bread. If it is too packed it needs a bit more cream. If it holds strong peaks and valleys that can be molded with spoons

it is ready. The first time through, solid is better than light. The beauty of a mousse or quenelle is in the balance between solid and moist.

In a large skillet or sauté pan bring 6 cups of water to a boil, add 2 teaspoons salt, and reduce the heat to a slight simmer. Using two soup spoons that have been standing in a glass of chilled water, form the quenelles: Scoop up the mousse in one, and with the other form an oval, spoon-shaped piece, and turn it gently into the simmering water. Return the spoons to the ice water, then repeat the process quickly, watching the water temperature

(*Recipe continued on page 72.*)

Quenelles of Salmon on Pasta with Tomato Bisque (continued)

to avoid a boil. Simmer the quenelles for 8 minutes. Gently roll them in the water as they become firm.

When they retain their shape lift out each quenelle in sequence with a slotted spoon and place gently on a rack to dry. At this point they may be frozen or refrigerated. When ready for serving, roll them gently in a buttered skillet over low heat. Pour I cup of the tomato bisque and the sherry gently into the same skillet and allow them to warm together. Spoon the quenelles onto serving plates filled with the cooked pasta. Pour the remaining tomato bisque over all and garnish with parsley.

SUPPORTING RECIPES

SUPPORTING RECIPES

GREEN MAYONNAISE

1 tablespoon lemon juice
1 egg (or 2 yolks for thicker mayonnaise)
1 tablespoon prepared mustard
Salt and pepper to taste
1¼ cups olive oil, divided

1 cup fresh watercress, washed and dried (or cooked,
 drained spinach)
1 tablespoon ground fines herbs

In a food processor fitted with the cutting blade, add the lemon juice, egg, mustard, salt and 1 tablespoon of olive oil. Process for 1 minute. Using a slow drip of oil from a measuring cup or the processor's pusher tube with a drip hole, add the remaining oil very slowly while the processor is running.

Add the watercress and the fines herbs and process for 1 minute more. Adjust seasonings and serve.

GRAVLAX HORSERADISH MUSTARD SAUCE

3 tablespoons olive oil
1 tablespoon red wine vinegar
1 tablespoon prepared horseradish
¼ teaspoon salt

½ teaspoon ground white pepper
3 tablespoons prepared mustard
3 tablespoons minced dill

Combine all the ingredients except the dill, which is served on a shallow butter plate at the side for sprinkling over each serving.

Sauce Nantua

FOR THE SHRIMP BUTTER:
3 pounds whole shrimp, heads and tails included
2 sticks butter (1 cup), melted

FOR THE BÉCHAMEL SAUCE:
2 tablespoons butter
2 tablespoons flour
1 cup warm milk
Salt and pepper
¼ teaspoon paprika
¼ teaspoon cayenne pepper
1 egg yolk
½ cup clam juice (or fish stock)
Tabasco sauce to taste (optional)

Peel the shrimp, preserving the shells, heads, feet and debris. Reserve the shrimp meat for some other purpose. On a flat baking sheet crisp the shells for 5 to 10 minutes in an oven preheated to 450°F. Turn the bits with a spatula and do not allow the shells to burn.

In a processor bowl place the shrimp bits, cover with the melted butter and process for 30 seconds, stopping and scraping as necessary. Spoon this creamed butter and shrimp paste into a saucepan and reheat gently. Repeat the blender process, and then finely strain the entire mixture into a small bowl. Stir occasionally as it cools to maintain the homogeneity of the butter.

Make a béchamel by forming a roux from the butter and flour in a small saucepan over low heat. When the flour is completely absorbed, add the milk and continue whisking over very low heat until the mixture thickens. Adjust the salt and pepper, add the paprika and cayenne, then whisk in the egg.

To 1 cup of béchamel add ½ cup clam juice and 4 to 5 tablespoons of the shrimp butter. Warm over low heat, stirring constantly, until thoroughly incorporated and the correct thickness is achieved. Test for seasoning, and add Tabasco sauce if desired.

Quick White Wine Sauce for Poaching

2 tablespoons chopped green onions
Salt and pepper
1 cup white wine
¼ cup fish stock (or clam juice)
1½ tablespoons butter, sliced small

1 tablespoon each butter and flour
½ cup sour cream (or heavy cream)
Additional ½ cup white wine, or less to reach desired
  consistency

This cooking liquid is the simplest medium for poaching fish, either whole or steaks or fillets, and then building a light wine sauce.

Sprinkle the green onions around the bottom of a buttered ovenproof dish. Lightly salt and pepper the fillets or steaks and lay them in the dish without overlapping. Add the wine and fish stock and dot each piece of fish with the butter slices. Add enough wine or water to almost reach the top of the fillets. Poach the fish according to the recipe.

After the fish is done, remove and keep warm. Strain and reduce the cooking liquid to ½ cup. In a small saucepan, form a roux with 1 tablespoon each butter and flour. Remove from the heat and incorporate the cream by whisking. Over low heat, slowly dribble the additional white wine into the mixture, stirring constantly until the desired consistency is reached. Adjust for taste with salt and pepper.

Fish Fumet (Fish Stock from Trimmings)

2 pounds fish heads, skin, bones, tails and fins
3 tablespoons vegetable oil
½ cup sliced onions
⅓ cup sliced carrots
½ cup thinly sliced celery root

5 cups white wine
5 cups water
1 bay leaf
⅓ cup chopped parsley
Salt and pepper to taste

Leave the scales on the skin of the fish and you will notice a thicker, more glutinous fish stock, which is of value in thickening sauces and flavoring other dishes.

In a large Dutch oven heat the oil and cook the onions, carrots and celery lightly until they begin to color. Add the wine, water, bay leaf, parsley, salt and pepper and fish parts and bring to a boil. Skim any foam from the liquid, and reduce to a simmer for 1 hour. Strain through cheesecloth and allow to cool. This *fumet poisson* may be clarified for use in aspics, or is easily frozen in 1-cup units and kept for months.

Tomato Bisque

½ cup thinly sliced onions
2 tablespoons olive oil
4 cups tomatoes, chopped, juice reserved
¼ teaspoon dried thyme
¼ teaspoon ground cayenne
1 bay leaf, crumbled

½ teaspoon each salt and pepper
2 cloves of garlic, crushed
2 cups fish stock as needed (or vegetable stock)
⅓ cup cream
Dry sherry to taste

In a large saucepan over low heat soften the onions in the oil for 10 minutes, but do not allow the onions to brown. Add the chopped tomatoes and juice and stir, allowing the tomatoes to soften in the heat for 3 minutes.

Add the herbs, seasonings and garlic and simmer over low heat for 30 minutes, stirring occasionally, and adding enough stock to maintain the desired consistency.

To create a bisque, add the cream and whisk carefully over low heat for 5 minutes. Add a splash of dry sherry and adjust the salt and pepper.

Court Bouillon with White Wine

4 cups white wine
4 cups water
1 cup thinly sliced onions
2 celery ribs with greens, thinly sliced
3 tablespoons chopped parsley

1 teaspoon dried thyme
2 bay leaves, crushed
1 tablespoon salt
1 teaspoon white peppercorns

This simple bouillon is called "court" because it is short, and does not contain the extenders of meat or fish that are found in the "larger" versions. The court bouillon should be cooked for half an hour or so, and then allowed to cool before the introduction of fish, particularly whole fish whose skin may split if placed in boiling liquid.

In a large pot combine all the ingredients except the peppercorns and bring to a rolling boil, then reduce and simmer for a total of 1 hour. After about 45 minutes crack the peppercorns and add them to the court bouillon, not allowing them to cook more than 12 minutes. Allow the court bouillon to cool, then strain and reserve for use.

Red wine may be substituted. In that case it is customary to add 2 cups of carrots, and black peppercorns may be substituted.

Fish Velouté Sauce

1 tablespoon butter
1 tablespoon flour
1 cup clam juice (or fish stock)

1 egg yolk, slightly beaten
Salt and pepper

In a small pan soften the butter over very low heat. Add the flour and stir constantly for 4 to 5 minutes until the butter bubbles, forming a roux. Do not allow the roux to color from the heat. Slowly pour in the clam juice, whisking constantly until the velouté forms. Add salt and pepper to taste. Remove from the heat and whisk in the egg yolk, stirring constantly. Return briefly to the heat until the sauce thickens. Remove and adjust the seasonings to taste.

BRIOCHE PASTRY

3 tablespoons dry yeast
1½ tablespoons warm milk
1 teaspoon sugar
4 cups flour

1½ tablespoons salt
12 tablespoons butter, chilled and cut to sugar-cube size
4 eggs, slightly beaten
⅓ cup milk, or more

Mix the yeast, warm milk and sugar in a small bowl and allow the yeast to proof for 5 minutes.

In a large processor bowl combine the flour and salt and blend briefly. Using the processor in 1-second bursts, add the butter cubes a few at a time until all the cubes are flaked.

In a large bowl combine the eggs and ⅓ cup milk and mix well. Add the yeast mixture and stir. Add this combination to the flour in the processor bowl and combine using short bursts, adding a bit more milk if necessary to form a soft dough.

Allow the dough to rest in the processor bowl for 10 minutes. Process the dough again for 30 seconds, then turn out onto a floured working surface. Knead the dough 22 strokes, then place in a large bowl. Cover the bowl and allow the dough to rise to twice its size in a cool, draft-free area. This should take about 45 minutes.

Deflate the dough and fold it, and repeat the folding three times. Then cover and allow it to rise to twice its size. When ready, punch down the dough and roll out to ¼-inch thickness and cut to shape. This dough can be chilled first, punched down, then wrapped tightly and refrigerated for several days. This recipe makes 1½ pounds of dough, sufficient for the coulibiac russe.

CULINARY PROCEDURES ILLUSTRATED

GRAVLAX

1.

Cut off the head and tail sections of the dressed and scaled salmon, leaving a 2-pound centercut, or "darne."

2.

From a midline incision down the spine fillet both sides, leaving the spine and all bones to be discarded. Use kitchen pliers to remove any other bones remaining in the meat.

3.

With the skin sides down, sprinkle half of the salt-sugar-pepper mixture evenly over the exposed meat of each fillet.

4.
Place one fillet, skin side down, in a shallow glass or earthenware dish, and cover completely with a thick layer of the dill, freshly chopped to release its bouquet.

5.
Place the second fillet, skin side up, over the first, arranging the top piece front to back if necessary to completely cover the underlying piece. Add all remaining dill and sugar-salt-pepper over and around the fish.

6.
Cover and wrap the fillets and the dish in aluminum foil, and place a wooden cutting board or other weight over the fish. Refrigerate for 48 hours, pouring off the fluid each day. To serve, cut the slices away from the skin on a slight bias as with smoked salmon.

FORMING THE NOISETTES OF SALMON

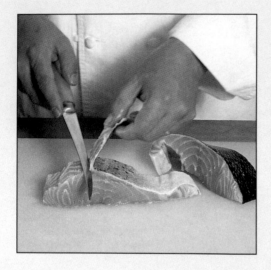

1.
Lay the large salmon steaks flat on a cutting board. With the tip of a sharp knife cut away the skin and then separate the steak into its two flanks. Remove the center bone and discard. Search the meat for smaller bones, which should also be discarded.

2.
Marinate each piece of the fish in the egg and olive oil mixture for 20 minutes.

3.
Remove the fish from the marinade and roll lightly in a bowl containing the flour and peppers, coating all sides of the fish.

4.

Working on a flat surface, begin at the larger end of the fish flank, and carefully coil it around itself like a rope until you reach the tip. Pin the tip of the fish with a bamboo skewer that is long enough to pierce through to the farthest end of the thickest section of the salmon, and out the other side.

5.

In a small saucepan melt the butter and allow it to color slightly. Add the noisettes and over medium heat baste and brown the fish, turning as necessary to achieve a uniform brown coloring.

6.

Remove the skewers from the cooled noisettes. Spoon the lemon juice over them and garnish with lemon slices and fried parsley.

BUILDING THE COULIBIAC

1.

Make 1½ pounds of brioche dough using 4 cups of flour and allow the dough to rest. (*See recipe on page 82.*)

2.

Roll out half the dough into a rectangle 12 x 8 inches by ¼-inch thick, and place this pastry base on an oiled baking sheet.

3.

Spoon half of the rice mixture into the center of the pastry, and arrange in a rectangle shape, leaving a 1-inch apron of open space around the interior perimeter of the pastry.

4.
Spoon half of the salmon flakes into a layer over the rice, and press the mixtures together lightly. Continue with alternate layers, pressing down between each. Cover the final layer with the mushroom, egg and velouté mixture.

5.
Roll out the remaining dough into a rectangle of 18 x 10 inches by ¼-inch thick. Brush the edges of the dough base with the egg and milk mixture and then gently lower the lid into place. Seal the edges firmly together with the back of a fork.

6.
Trim off any excess pastry, and roll out and cut the excess to create Russian forest motifs of vines and leaves and figs. Cut a vent hole in the center of the pastry roof, and insert a foil funnel. Apply the designs, and brush over all with the egg and milk. Cook in an oven preheated to 400°F for 40 minutes, using a foil cover to avoid burning toward the end.

STUFFING A SALMON FILLET WITH SHRIMP MOUSSE

1.

Remove all bones from a fillet side, then skin the fillet. Divide the fillet into two long halves from head to tail, and cut each section into 4-inch-long serving pieces, about 2½ inches wide and 1 inch thick.

2.

On a large cutting board lay each serving piece flat, and using the flat side of a large cleaver and a kitchen hammer, tap the cleaver to flatten the fillet to the new shape of about 7 inches long x 4 inches wide.

3.

Beat the egg whites in a chilled bowl (copper is best) with 1 tablespoon ice water until they reach soft peaks. Add the whites to a processor bowl with the shrimp and grated cheese and combine for 10 seconds.

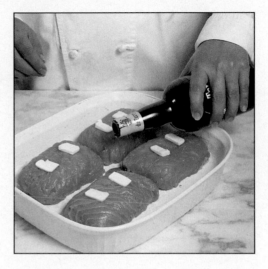

4.

In a large mixing bowl, fold the rice mixture into the shrimp mixture, adding enough bread crumbs to form a patty that will hold its shape.

5.

Using about ¾-cup each, form the shrimp mousse into small rectangles about 3 x 4 inches by ¾-inch tall. Place these on a baking sheet, and fit each block of mousse with an overlapped salmon fillet, tucked in at the head and tail. Refrigerate.

6.

Place all the stuffed salmon, fish side up, in a buttered roasting pan and add the butter and olive oil to the pan with an extra sliver of butter on top of each fillet. Pour the sherry around the edges and cook for 20 minutes in a 400°F oven, basting occasionally. Cover if necessary to prevent scorching.

INDEX